# WORDS LIKE WATER

POETRY *by* KIRSTEN MORGAN

Written and illustrated by Kirsten Morgan
social | @kirstenmorgan.poetry

Edited by Gabrielle Morgan
social | @gab.morgann

Cover Design by Mariah Danielsen of Wander Design Co.
social | @wanderdesignco // website | wanderdesignco.com

# ACKNOWLEDGEMENTS

To my Mom and Dad, thank you– for all the ways you have saved me, encouraged me, carried me, pushed me, supported me, and taught me. No combination of words could ever summarize how thankful I am for the love you have for me, for each other, and for our family. The two of you are a living reflection of your faith and are a picture of what it means to be steadfast. Thank you.

To Ginger, thank you– for always showing up, for cheering me on in every season, and for believing in this dream of mine when I wasn't even sure if I believed in it. You are the very definition of loyalty and friendship. Thank you.

To Gabby, thank you– for pouring your knowledge into this book and your confidence into me. Words Like Water is better because of you. You are gifted and I am thankful for your willingness to share those gifts and this experience with me. Thank you.

To everyone that believed in my words long before I did, thank you. I am only brave enough to share them because your encouragement drowns out my self-doubt. Thank you.

Dear Reader,

I am so glad that you are here! I would like to begin by explaining that writing is something that I do to help me process the big and small things in my life. Through every season I've lived, there were few consistencies, but writing was always one of them. As a child, sleepovers with my best friend consisted of writing elaborate stories on sheets of notebook paper and carefully tucking them into binders for safe keeping, only to be revisited years later. As a teenager, I doodled thoughts in spiral notebooks for no one else to see. As a young adult, my computer was a place for studying, journaling, and writing little poems. As a way to find healing after surviving an abusive relationship, I shared my words with others for the first time in hopes that my journey may help someone else with theirs. Now, my living room bookshelves are filled with journals of scribbled poems, diaries from my travels, and ink-smeared prayers. Writing has given me an outlet for expression, for celebration, and for healing. Sharing these words with others is frightening and uncomfortable, but I've learned that I grow best when I challenge myself to stretch beyond the borders of my comfort zone. With that said, this is me wholeheartedly pursuing this outlet that I find purpose in. I hope that by sharing these vulnerable parts of me, I will feel free and you will feel seen.

Thank you so much for being here.

With Love,

Kirsten

# FALLING. CRASHING. RISING. GROWING.

These four verbs encapsulate what I believe to be the lifecycle of love (and life too, probably). The fall, accidental. The crash, inevitable. But the rising and the growing? Those are purposeful. Those are chosen.

What this lifecycle looks like for each of us, individually and in relationship, is widely variable. Some couples fall, crash, and rise up together, growing to be more unified. Some fall, crash, and must rise on their own, apart from the relationship they once knew. We are all faced with challenges– in and out of love. I believe that our response to those challenges is often more significant in our stories than the challenge itself. While a reignited love deserves celebrating, I believe that the individuals who choose to rise and grow independently deserve just as much celebration! So, here is my cake and card in celebration of the growing that we do– in relationship, in community, and, most importantly, internally.

# FALLING

*Falling, I think, is the most accidental of things we do in love. The fall is natural, exhilarating, and brings out the best in each person. Fighting the fall out of self-preservation can be anxiety inducing, but the fall itself is everything. Each fall is deeply personal, but the rush is universally understood. These poems are about the fall– the giddiness and the ease of new love. These poems were written from a place of bursting at the seams over discovering the heights of happiness in unexpected places.*

# At First Sight

A handshake between strangers.
A polite exchange of names.
Organic from inception,
Though different than I imagined.
A face I'd only begun to learn,
But somehow so familiar
As if we'd known each other since our youth
Instead of after years of our own weathering.

# MMXIX

# Tell Me

Tell me about your favorite color,

The guy you hate at work,

Your major in college.

Then when we're done with small talk,

Tell me about your best day ever

And your worst.

Tell me about the song that reminds you of your dad

And the recipe that tastes like home.

Tell me about your greatest heartache,

Your wildest dream,

Your proudest moment.

Tell me about that old truck in your yard

And how you feel about me.

# Revival

The parts of me long thought dead,
Simply had been sleeping.
Flatlined to faint beats,
Now bounding in my chest.
This buried heart has been
Resurrected.

# July

Sunlight danced through open windows,
A familiar record played loud for neighbors to hear,
Bacon sizzled in the kitchen,
And we held that hug for far too long
As if afraid that we'd lose each other again
If ever we let go.

# Happy Tears

I'd never known what it was like to
Cry from happiness
Until you told me you loved me that night
And I said it back to you.
Then there it was,
A tear steamed out from my eye
And happiness
At the same time.

# Summer

Laughter rings out from your lungs
Like the music from that old boombox.
Freckles pop up
One after another,
On your shoulders and
On my nose.
Warm from the sun,
Our skin slowly cools as
The day melts into
Another firefly evening.
We stay up way too late,
Wide-awake dreaming
That life will always look this way.

# *Together*

A best friend and lover,
We found in each other.
Together, it all makes sense.

# *Labor Day*

Our love is
Golden and amber,
Warm, like sun-kissed skin
After a day on the water.

Wild and uninhibited–
Like climbing up on the roof,
Hands slipping on shingles,
Just to get a better look at the stars
On a summer night.

*You*

Like waking up from a nap on a plane,
Realizing I'm finally home.
A half dozen times across the ocean.
Al fresco dinners with a view.
I've tasted the world,
But came up still searching
For what I found in you.

# Falling

I fell for you

Not because of what you do

What you have

How you look

Or what you wear.

I fell for you in the way you smiled at me

On back roads to nowhere,

And how you laughed

When I got scared in four-wheel drive;

How you cleaned up spilled wine

Without anger,

And how your heart felt

Beating next to mine.

# Guiding Lights

Faintly illuminated outlines
Gently rocking in that little fishing boat,
Eyes turned upwards.
The sun had melted away,
But cascading through the open sky,
The stars remained–
Guiding lights above.

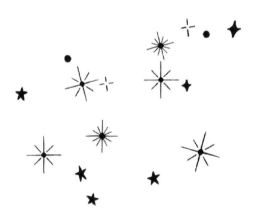

# Side by Side

I followed you into the cold creek water,

Where a younger you once played.

With each step, I shivered,

But never glanced back

And, I guess, that day

Is when I decided

Wherever you went, I wanted to go too.

# My Confession

I saw you linger over that same grainy photo
Each time you held my phone.

Hair tied off in a braid, I sat,
Wearing the most genuine smile I've ever known.
*"Happy"* captioned the screen.

I saw you study it, no doubt, wondering
What made me so happy that day.
The only secret I ever kept–
That smile on my face
Was from you.

# All-Consuming

We drank each other in
Like a shared peach drink on the open water,
With no drops left at the end of the day–
Just an empty bottle.

# Christmas Stockings

You told me you'd never had a Christmas stocking

So I got one for you,

And your dog, too.

I wanted you to know that

Christmases with me

Would always mean there'd be a stocking for you by my tree.

The two of you,

Family.

# Contact Tracing

Quarantined,
But we didn't mind.
Socially distanced
In our own paradise.
Away from it all,
Together.

# Incoming Call

Some days you call me three times in a row,
Just because you want to.
There is nothing new to say,
We just rest in each other's company.

# My Valentine

This time last year
I sat, wrapped in a blanket,
Writing poems about missing you.

Now, I sit,
Looking at the blanket ladder
You had made just for me,

And I know
That as safe as those blankets make me feel,
I'm even safer next to you.

# All I Ask

I didn't ask for you to save me
Or to heal any of my brokenness in me.
I didn't ask you to fix me
Or carry any weight besides your own.
All I ask is for you to be you,
Wholeheartedly you
And let me be me,
Wholeheartedly me,
Together, a team.
Individually, free.

# Muse

I loved you
With every part of me.
And that, alone,
Is poetry.

# Take the Jump

Frightening.

Just the thought of falling in love...

Reckless abandon for the safety of your heart.

Will it all end in a crash or will my parachute deploy?

A rocky shoreline leers below me.

I take the jump,

Relishing in the adrenaline as I soar,

Soaking in the beauty of the fall.

# CRASHING

*Falling in love is the easy part, but the cultivation of that love is not so accidental. It requires effort, a trial and error of learning another. Any number of scenarios can cause a love to fall from its peak, but the crashing is invariably painful. These poems are written from a place of confusion, frustration, sadness, and anger. There is difficulty in reconciling all that emerges when a relationship nears an end, in coming to terms with closure despite "what could have been." This person once so perfect for you, a stranger now and the person you were with them, now a stranger to you too. Never easy, but sometimes necessary– the crash, a storm that clears a new path. While painful, I believe the crashing to be devastatingly beautiful as our most raw, most vulnerable self surfaces here. The emotions vary widely from moment to moment, day to day. After the crash, we find what remains underneath. These poems are my reckoning with that reality.*

# *Perspective*

You liked your coffee strong and black;
I liked mine smoothed over with vanilla cream.
You always waited on the bad news to come;
I told you to expect good things.

# Succulents

I had the best intentions,
But drowned them slowly
With outpoured love too frequent.
I guess my heart was made
For so much more
Than once a month affection.

# The Answer Was No

I wanted to go west

Or north

Or south

Or anywhere.

But you wanted to

Stay

Right

Here.

I felt my heart break a little

When we cancelled those flights.

I wondered then if two hearts

Made so differently could still

Be made for one another.

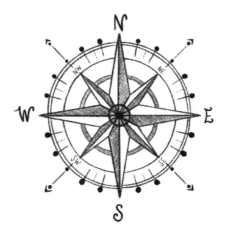

*Alaska*

A wild heart, you claimed.
We shared the same
Drive for adventure,
Thirst for something new.

You lacked opportunity,
But dreamed of Denali.
Of vast open spaces, and
An aurora view.

Two roundtrip flights.
Our dream trip, I planned,
*"The first thing I've been excited about in years"*
Turned into you deciding that we simply
Can't.

It's a lot of money, and
The timing isn't great.
I don't want to rush it,
Just cancel the flights.
Maybe one day,
Maybe some other time.

A new lesson,
I've since found out to be true:
Some people talk,
Some people do.

# Next Steps Should Not Be Ultimatums

You wanted a "For Sale" sign in my yard
And boxes moved from my home to yours.

I wanted to watch sunsets and count stars
From the front porch I'd share with you.

We wanted the same thing, it seemed,
But you wanted me to sacrifice it all,
Just to be your roommate.

# The War Within You

Your head and your heart
War violently against each other,
Like Hatfield's and McCoy's
And other age-old tales of feuding.
A forever kind of love, some kids in the backseat
Or this lifetime of a bachelor–
Whatever you want, whenever you please.
You can't have them both,
No matter how hard you try.
And maybe that's the reason
You can't sleep at night.

# Crabgrass

Quick-tempered man,
You always warned me
As if admitting your shortcomings
Excused them.
There's work that needs done,
The searching out and digging up of roots
In your garden bed of weeds.
Admitting its presence within
Won't keep crabgrass from
Choking out every good thing that's been planted.

# Your Recliner

The two of us
Sandwiched in that recliner of yours.
The only chair you owned,
The most comfortable place I could have known.
Unsure of who's leg is who's by the end of the show,
Just comfortable sitting there,
Together.

How then did that chair so quickly become a
Prison of discomfort?
*"Can you slide over?"*
*"You're sitting on me."*
Suddenly unable to reach the remote,
Unable to breathe–
Did we grow overnight?
Or did we just grow apart?

# Never Enough

Three course meals
Made from scratch.
And all those Sunday chores.
Grocery shopping
To ease your stress.
*"Don't worry, I'll clean the mess."*
All of me, an endless pour
Just to wake up to
*"I can't do this anymore."*

# Crashing

A home, I built in you.
I found rest inside your walls.
Your smile, the oven that brought all my meals to life.
Your arms, my blanket at night.

I'll never forget the day
That the earth quaked with anger,
Waking us all from our sleep.
There were warnings we'd ignored
Until the fault line cracked our foundation.

I thought it could be saved but
Seven days went by before
My home came crashing down,
Burying me in the rubble.

# Twenty-Four Miles

Each night I reached for my keys,
You'd lean forward in that well-worn chair,
Sleepy eyes gazing upwards at mine
*"You're not staying?"*

Twenty-four miles grew between us
And I'd miss you all the way home.

So on that last rainy Saturday
As you gathered your things,
I asked you the same
With heavy eyes, swollen with tears
*"You're not staying?"*

You kissed my forehead, closed the door.
Twenty-four miles grew between us.
Did you miss me all the way home?

# Provision

Capsized and drowning,
All I could do was cry out.
The three of you,
Never far away,
Heard and came racing to save me.

One held the boat, calmly steering.
One threw a raft, reeling me in.
And one dried the water spilled out from my lungs,
As I breathed in and no longer gasped for air.

# New Grocery Store

I cried in the grocery store

Over protein bars and frozen pizzas

That didn't look the same as the ones we used to buy.

Every single thing is different now.

Even breakfasts on the go

And last-minute dinners after a long day at work.

# Good Doctor

I came to you
Cheeks flushed and tear-stained
Words choked out
One at a time.

> "I'm glad you're here"
> and not
> "What's wrong?"

How nice to see
Your starched white coat
Has not ironed out your heart's softness.

Five deep breaths outside each day
Was all you asked of me.

A sigh of relief.
That's all?

I'm used to giving
    So.
    Much.
    More.

# Mother's Day

Cheerful smiles at a church house,
Candies offered,
And a rose.

They don't know
Those aren't for me.
They just see
A face lined with sunspots,
Skinny jeans that tell my age.
Assumptions made:
*"Happy Mother's Day!"*

A familiar sting deep within the body
that's never carried another.

They don't know that
He's gone, and with him,
The dream of squishy babes
And a celebration on this day.

# I Wrote This Five Days Before We Broke Up

A fickle thing:
Sand,
Sometimes warm and comforting.
A rest stop, escape, and a paradise
All in one.

And later warmth escapes,
The sand left
Hard, cold–
Like ice with its broken shards of shell
Making their way into my skin.

A good place for a time,
Perhaps,
But not for a home.
Learning that you, my dear, are
A man of sand
Is the saddest thing I've ever come to know.

# Gut Feeling

I wrestled my own mind.
Days turned into months.
A gut feeling
That I argued with
And couldn't accept.
That goodbye would be choked out
From my mouth,
A death to what could have been–
An ending to what was.

# Casseroles and Cheesecakes

There's an unsettled darkness within you
That made me feel like I should save you,
Like if I could love you well enough,
I could heal the broken parts of you.
But casseroles and cheesecakes proved not to be enough,
When you would reach past me
For another drink
Every time.

# Secret Book

There's a secret book of prayers
Tucked away on my bookshelf,
Unassuming but full.
Inside, scribbled heart cries often smeared–
A graveyard of fallen tears.
Words of vulnerability, pleading with God
Make him whole.
Make him happy.
Draw him near.

# Swatches Still on the Counter

You couldn't commit
To a paint color for the walls of your living room.
So why did I think you meant it when you said you were
Committed to me?

# My Brain Forgets You're Gone

I dreamed of you again last night.
You met me somewhere I didn't know,
But I knew it was you
By those little bumps under your left eye,
And how your eyes changed colors
In the light,
And the way you didn't seem to hurt at all
When you told me goodbye.

# Sudden Death

Sometimes I forget
You didn't die
The day we said goodbye.
I mourned for days.
Like sudden death–
The life I knew ripped away
But there was no grave.
And when I remember that
You're still out there,
Living
Without me,
I'm undone by grief
All over again.
Life, sometimes,
More painful than death.

# Insomnia

wide awake
2:30 am
racing thoughts
neural fire
pen to paper
scribbled ink

# Late Night

It's weird,

How it all comes rushing back at random.

All day, I'm fine

And then

My head hits the pillow and you're not there.

Like, okay, I get it–

I was wrong:

We weren't meant for each other.

Most hours I'm at peace with that reality

Then 11 comes around,

And then 12,

And then 2,

And I'm still just lying here thinking about you,

Wondering how something so perfect

Faded into this.

How two hearts so connected

Managed to drift,

Leaving me lost in a sea

Of my own salty tears.

# Straw Wrappers

You tore my heart apart
Like the straw wrappers
You'd always twist into tiny paper balls
While sitting in that familiar red booth,
Patiently waiting on Mexican food.
Just something to occupy your time,
Fully entranced for a while
Then cast aside–
A mess left for someone else to clean.

# Outlook

I'll live in my mindset of abundance
You never understood.
And you keep living in cynical belief
That this world is full,
But nothing's good.

# Impasse

A dead end disguised as a pathway.

A closed door that I won't try to walk through.

A crime scene taped,

**Do Not Enter.**

You're my forbidden fruit.

CRIME SCENE - DO NOT ENTER    CRIME SC

# Rhetorical

And when you find another,

I wonder

Will she make you dinner

So you won't eat beef jerky as a meal?

Will she drive back and forth for you,

Never expecting the same amount of give?

Will she always save your Mama a piece of dessert

Because she wants her to know she is loved?

Will she hang your clothes the way you like,

Or will you take the hangers,

Readjusting her efforts?

Will she love you as well as I did?

And will you take her love for granted

Just as you did mine?

# You'll Search Forever

By your own admission,
Something's always been missing.
*"I've been unhappy my whole life."*
Oh, my dear, you'll search forever
And never be satisfied.

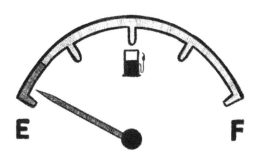

# Introspection

You watched a friend go west at age thirty.
You asked no questions,
Simply insisted that
He's too old for wandering.
It's time for settling.
He just needs a good girl back home.

It's been a year now and he found his way back,
A new mortgage sits in his name.

And you?
You're posting pictures in a mirror, and
Entertaining another man's bride,
Forgetting that you, too, are growing
In age not maturity.
An ironic disconnection,
Your great lack of introspection.

# Recollection

|

Trust came easily this time
And I'm not really sure why.
I just believed we shared
A connection for the ages,
A forever love in its early stages.
But now I'm alone,
Driving myself home,
Scream singing about things remembered too well.
I hope one day I'll be numb to your memory
And that my senses won't allow you to haunt me
From the grave of our love deceased.
But, for now, the smell of your body wash still lingers in my mind
And the sound of country music gets me every time.
One single note and I'm back
Driving your boat, hair blowing in the breeze,
And I look over to find you laughing with me,
Recording each moment, frozen in time—
You and me, so full of life.
I hope one day I'll be better than I am right now,
But today I'm simply unwell.
Today, I guess, I remember too well.

# Supporting Beams

I guess that's why this time hurt so bad.

I was scared to let you love me;

I was scared to let you in.

The last person allowed access to me wreaked havoc within,

But how wrong it'd be for you to pay for another man's sins.

It's okay that our hearts turned out to be different.

Constructions aren't meant to all be the same.

I just wish you told me you before I let you tear down my walls,

Before I signed my name to agree to your remodel.

Supporting beams came crashing down

In your careless demolition.

# Lies I Tell Myself

If I had known it would end like this, I would have walked away.

If I could go back and change what happened, I wouldn't hesitate.

I'm not angry that you ruined a beautiful thing.

I'm not sad that our friendship ended this way.

I'm not more at peace now that you've drifted away.

I'm not conflicted with my emotions every day.

I'm fine, really, I'm okay.

# *Everything*

Mama says there's good things coming,
Someone better for me.
I try to just smile
But remember, all the while,
That, for a time, it was you and me.
We were the good things.

# Loneliness

Better for loneliness to creep in for a moment
In a house of only me,
Than for it to reside within my mind,
While you sit right next to me.

# Collateral Damage

Family recipes exchanged but
One day they'll forget my name.
It's hard to say goodbye to
What you thought would last forever.
Give your aunt a hug for me;
Your best friend's daughter, too.
Heartbreak comes in many forms,
Like saying *"see you later"*
Not knowing it's not true.

# Slow Pour

A slow pour of hot coffee
Is so much more satisfactory
Than careless dumping,
Sticky splashes staining the counter.
I suppose love is the same way:
The good stuff eased into,
A slow but steady hand,
Taking care to not spill
Hot coffee on fragile skin,
For burns take a long time to heal.

# Forever

Your best friend once told me
I'm the only girl to ever meet your Mama.
I found rest in Christmas presents exchanged,
Easter dinner with those that share your name,
Believing our story would one day pass down
To little babes whose names you'd already planned.

You told me you loved me first,
So I thought it must be true.
Even now, I know that
It was true for me and it was true for you.

I suppose I became too comfortable,
Believing these words were more than
Finite expressions set to expire–
A shelf life found to be much shorter than forever.

# Moving On

You're my childhood home—
Walls bare and empty,
No longer meant for me.
Instead of in my arms,
I'll hold you now
In memory.

# American Dream

The manicured lawns of my neighbors.

The perfect mirage they see of me.

Each plant well-watered,

Weeds plucked from view.

But behind each closed door,

What reality rings true?

Picture perfect displays

Projected for all to see,

But a medicine cabinet unseen

Helps ease the pain of

Living this American dream.

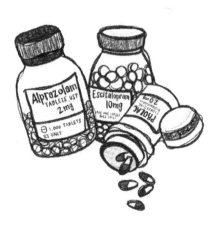

# Shallow

Shallow love is not for me.
I'd rather brave the unknown
In search of something real.
A shipwrecked heart
Lost in the deep–
Better to drown
Than to be left wishing for more,
Sitting safely in the shallow.

# RISING

Rising, I believe, is about more than a decision made on an isolated occasion to stand up from whatever hardship knocked you down. I believe rising is an ongoing decision, a culmination of an infinite number of choices made each day. It is the process of coming to a point of closure and reaching a point of acceptance for the moments that molded us, both beautifully and tragically. It is the recognition of your own intrinsic value despite the invalidation you may have received from others. It is the moving forward and moving on that we must do with any life change we face. At times, it is simply an acknowledgment of conflicting emotions as you navigate these changes– the parts of your heart still hurting, the parts of your mind now free. In the dainty balance of choosing self-love and looking externally towards something bigger than ourselves, little by little, we rise.

# Love

The bravest thing any one of us can do,
I wholeheartedly believe.

Reckless, at its core:
To selflessly choose another–
To trust and learn and sacrifice,
All the while,
Risking ruin.

We've all been injured.
Some wounds mended by time,
Some still raw and bleeding–
And we keep coming back for more,
Like love is what we were made for.

# Losing You, Finding Me

I thought it'd kill me,
Just the thought of
Losing you.
Oh, but,
Losing you,
It turns out,
Was just the first stop
On the map to
Finding me.

# Please Exit Here

And if he wants to leave,

Open the door

And watch him go.

There's good in goodbyes

To those not made for your soul.

# Excessive Benevolence

I believe in sacrifice
But not of all of me.
I've made myself smaller
For the comfort of others,
A lamb to the slaughter I will be
No longer.

# The Cruelty of Apathy

I missed you more

When you were still mine.

Your apathetic drift,

How quietly cruel,

Kept me in chronic upheaval.

I rest easy now.

It wasn't you;

It was peace,

All along,

That I needed.

# Awakening

You may not have been sure of me,
But now, I'm sure of myself.
I'm better off without you and
Your unending internal distress.

# In My Bones

You once called me a victim
Because I did not accept
The disrespect you gave.
That's the day
I should have walked away
Instead of fighting for something
Not worth restoring.
If ever you believed me to be a victim,
You never knew me at all.
Overcoming is in my DNA.
Surviving is in my bones.

# Dog-Eared Pages

Why is it that our brains tell stories of all the good things,
But leave out the moments of sitting next to another,
Invalidated and feeling lonely?

Why does my brain fail to remind me of the times I pondered goodbye,
Believing there's no way that I could feel misunderstood for a lifetime?

But no.
She flips right to the page of cabin days,
Movie nights snuggled up together.
She tells stories of the happiness,
Tales of shared laughter.
But what about your curated stress with your friends and with me,
Like deep down every face is your enemy?
What about the pages of the days I didn't eat–
You needed space but haven't seen me all week?

My brain tells of what it wishes to remember,
Hiding away pain–
Idealizing is simpler.
No matter the flashbacks and the memories within,
There's more room for me now than there's ever been.
There's peace for the taking I wouldn't have otherwise known.
There's good that has come from this chapter's close.

# Remnants

In the dividing up of things–
Of all our memories,
You left your t-shirts hanging
In my closet, tucked among
Things I always wear.
Comforted in my heartache,
A part of you still resided here.
Stored away now in a bottom drawer,
They rest amongst the long forgotten.
Removed from my weekly rotation,
I don't sleep in them anymore.

# Giving Myself Grace

One day I'll be able to do it;
I'll be able to remove you.
Our friendship ended long ago,
But there's a guilty pleasure–
A heart prick,
Every time I see your name.
That face I used to study so intently
Comes across on my feed, and
I'm reminded of my humanness.
We're strangers now, I suppose,
But I'm not yet ready for that permanent reality.

# If I'm Honest

Numb souls don't grow, they say.
But sometimes I'd rather fade away,
Put my mind to bed for a while.
I'll try again tomorrow.

# Amnesia

Memories:
Fuzzy,
Like the plotline of a skimmed-over book
From ninth grade.
I'm left questioning,
Was this the story of me or
Someone else along the way?
Disappeared moments,
Names and times escaped,
As if none of it was real.
But ever faintly,
I think I've lived this all before.
Am I dissociating or just merciful?
Protected in detachment,
This harrowed mind of mine:
Forgetful but kind.

# Patient Education

It's no coincidence, I know,
The title my name badge carries.
My days are filled with
Patient education
Of what to expect,
The process of healing.
Consistent, never linear.
Ups and downs
Over time,
And even when it hurts like hell,
Healing.

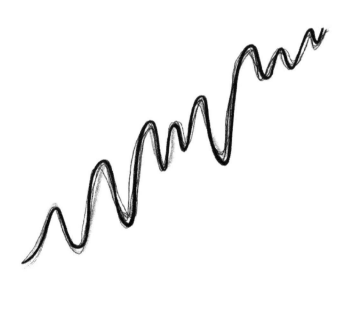

# I'm Proud of Myself

How do I know I've grown?
In endless ways,
But, most assuredly, because I do not crumble
At the sound of your name.

# Closure

And if you ever come to the place
Where you realize what you had,
Your epiphany will be much too late;
She's never coming back.

# My Name

Too often, people question why
My name is my own.
It's not given by another.
There was no power invested.
A surname, not a maiden name.
It's mine; I possess it.
There's no explanation owed,
But if you must know:
I prefer to be alone
If it ensures peace
Is all that resides with my home.

# Revelation

On that first date by the beach,
A butterfly danced all around us.
Each hike that we went on,
Each moment we shared,
Butterflies followed–
In my heart,
In the air.

They're my favorite,
I confided
And it became our thing.

And now,
When one flutters by,
I'm at peace
Knowing change is a good thing.

# Birthday Flowers

I bought myself a flower today,
A delphinium
In my favorite shade of blue.
I just couldn't walk past it at the nursery
Because it reminded me of
Roadside wildflowers in summertime,
And that I deserve pretty flowers on Mondays,
Not just on birthdays.

# Mantra

May the things and people
Not meant for me
Roll out with the tide,
Headed back to the sea.

# Yellow

Gone are the days
Where I reach past my favorite blouse,
To opt for something different
Because you told me you don't like yellow.

From now on,
I'll be goldenrod, waving wildly in a field.
I'll be a swallowtail, fluttering among the tulip trees.
I'll be a maple in autumn, sharing my leaves as a gift to the earth.
I'll be every shade of yellow I wish to be.

# Dopamine

The heart flutters.
The rush.
My lit-up screen.
An addiction to you,
Formed in my brain.

So when the texts came less frequent,
The calls hours late,
Anxiety waged war,
Causing physical pain.

The Saturday calls to make sure I'm still coming
Faded into changed plans,
Time spent with your buddies.

Our talks every night always made my day better,
But your moods of glass
Left me always awaiting
The next time you'd shatter.

Finally deciding,

I'll speak up, it's not fair–

I deserve to receive the same effort I give.

No surprise to me, but

You disagreed.


Withdrawal at first.

Now so much better.

Power, no more, to leave me unsettled.

The good times, so good.

The bad, not so much,

But that doesn't erase the joy in what was.


Thankful for what is,

Thankful for what was.

I'll depend on myself now for my dopamine rush.

# Estranged

I thought I'd miss you,
But I really haven't yet.
I think I'm just happy to be
Reunited with myself.

# *Reflection*

And when, one day, you meet another,
Please don't be gripped by fear.
I hope that even after heartbreak,
You'll love again, my dear.

# Rising

I find myself thinking about rising–
Wishing I could convey this notion that I'm like the others:

A lotus springing up from mud,

A phoenix from ashes,

But it would simply be untrue.

I'm just me–

Even still, rising

Though not quite as triumphantly.

My heart may sting,
But I laugh with sincerity,
Patiently awaiting a new day,
Knowing it may or may not be better than the last.

Even still, rising.

# Resilience

Forever fell apart,
But I didn't.

# *Happier*

"*You could be happier.*"

I didn't believe him at the time,
Until I found myself floating,
Tethered to sisters,
Kayaks rocking with the current
And our belly laughs.
I didn't worry if they were mad at me;
They just seemed glad to be
Tethered right next to me, too.

And he was right:
I was happier.

# Relief

I have nowhere to rush;
I have no place to be,
Except exactly where I want,
Exactly as I please.
I'm free to rest.
How nice to simply exist,
Apart from others' expectations.

# Remember

Rising from what's brought you down
Does not erase the pain you've had.
It does not mean that bad days cease–
No room here for toxic positivity.
There's good and there's bad.
Happy, sad.
Endless cliche pairings could be listed out.
The choosing of rising is not the dismissal of trial
But the purposeful effort given to move forward,
Even if on hands and knees,
Crawling towards better things.
Unseen obstacles still ahead,
Unlevel ground sinking in,
Inching onward,
Fighting to stand,
Believing it will all be worth it in the end.

# *Evergreen*

If not a love of evergreen,

Not a love for me.

Uninterested in changed feelings

With changed seasons,

The shedding of leaves and divvying up of belongings.

Consistently lush on

Summer nights,

Illuminated by the low hanging moon

And myrtle-hued foliage just as full on

Snowy mornings,

Carrying new weight, cold burdens.

A spruce in a forest full of oaks,

Decidedly, I'm not for deciduous love.

# GROWING

*Instead of viewing growth as a destination to arrive upon, I believe it should be viewed as a journey– birth to grave. Growth is the hard work put into heart work and is an ongoing practice, never ceasing. Growing, I know, extends far beyond just lessons from the earth, but I seem to learn best from natural things. In nature, plants are either growing or stagnant, flourishing or withering, living or dying. People, in a sense, are the same. Growing from our hardships is neither superficial nor unintentional. Growth and maturation require the pruning back of the dead. It calls for a willingness to dirty our hands, to dig to the root of the hurt underneath. It requires consistency and it requires care– the daily practice of cultivating our most healthy self. It requires challenging ourselves to be uncomfortable through changing seasons. And, perhaps, above all– it requires grace, patience, and compassion– with others and with ourselves. Growth is not the constant production of blooms. It is also the deepening of hidden roots and the shedding of dead leaves. These poems are written from my heart's continual pursuit of living a life filled with purpose, with peace, with gratitude, with learning, and with doing things that make me feel most alive. I hope these reflections encourage you to flourish wherever you are, in whatever season you find yourself in.*

# A Beautiful Thing

Even in this perpetual drought,
Still you choose to pour out,
Watering others in kindness,
Believing rain will one day come your way.

# Growing

More than pursuit of glowing,

Shining bright, the healing done for onlookers.

More internal–

The pruning back of

Growth stunting things.

Hands dirty from work,

Unsure when blooms will emerge.

Growth on its own terms.

Seasons of root development.

Seasons of full blooms.

Seasons of wilted leaves.

Growth is more than just

A display of the pretty things.

# Self-Love

Of all the people I've ever hurt in this world,
I've been most cruel to you.

I should have protected you,
Shielded you from harm,
Believed you when you hinted that something was wrong.
I should have chosen you,
But I always chose the others.
I should have built you up,
But I've let you break down over time.

An apology I owe,
But please know
I'm a work in progress and
I'm still learning
That self-love isn't selfish
When in the right dosage.

I'm sorry that you suffered through my deficiency.

# Wound Care

May there never come a time
Where you fester in
What could have been.

Grieve the life you thought you'd live.
It's human to feel pain.
Wounds heal from the inside out–
Keep it clean,
Wash it off,
Don't pick at your scabs.

One day– closed up,
Your scar will move like skin.
Forgotten injuries from before,
Dusted off knees
Running on fields they once cried on.

All because you made an effort to let yourself heal.
All because you saw value in your own
Wound care.

# A Letter to Myself

There is purpose for your pain,
For your stories,
For the memories you'd wish away.
There is a plan for the words
That dance tirelessly through your mind.
There is a reason for those words inside.
You just have to write them.

# *Relationship*

How sad that a people made for relationships have
Minimized its depth, confining it to mere romance.

Romantic relationship has its place,
Else there'd be no Valentine's Day.
But relationship abounds into much further territory:
Friendships and family,
Familiar faces at the grocery,
The tortoiseshell cat that greets you at the door, and
The person in the mirror you must learn to care for.
We've simplified relationship to the presence of a partner,
But the value of a person does not hinge on another,
On the presence or absence of someone to call your lover.

Singleness not synonymous with loneliness,
Marriage not the epitome of fulfillment.
No need for lawyers,
A great change in statistics
If vows to another were so idyllic.

Natural to hope for, to wish for,
But not all that there is in store.
I, too, like the idea of growing old with another,
But to grow together, we must also grow internal.
May we never become so centered
On a pursuit to find love,
We forget to find ourselves along the way.

# Congratulations!

I can celebrate the good things that happen to others,
Even though they don't happen for me.
Their success is not my defeat.
Our timelines do not compete.

# *Recalculating*

No matter how many wrong turns you seem to make,
No matter how many times you feel lost along the way,
May your spirit remain adventurous.
Find comfort in knowing
The joy is in the learning,
In the growing that we do.
The destination is so much sweeter
When about more than just a view.

# Ring by Spring

You could have married at twenty-one,
Like the others that you knew.
That nice boy from college, perhaps?
Unfulfilled–
It wasn't love.
But you'd be settled down by now, no doubt.

Even at that wide-eyed age,
You knew
A life like others was not one for you.

All these years,
They'd be lost.
The experience and heartbreak,
The learning and unlearning.
You'd have lost all your becoming.

You could've done just like the others,
But a great expense it'd be,
To undo all these years of growth.
Comparison's a thief.

# Unabridged

There are well-meaning people that say

>*"You'll find someone"*
>When I'm single and
>*"It's good to see you happy"*
>When I'm not.

Polite banter and a gracious smile
Are all I've ever offered,
But sometimes I just wish that they knew:

>I've been happy with another and
>I've been happy on my own.
>I've loved in a way that was freeing, but
>I've never felt as free
>As when boarding a plane of perfect strangers
>Headed towards the Middle East.

>I've shared seasons with another,
>Daily rhythms are no longer.
>But since I was seventeen,
>I've worked to build this life you see.
>The degrees, the job I always wanted,
>A house that I've made my home.
>My passport filled, but I'll find room for more
>Because these dreams live on despite those who walk out my door.

A woman, complete, all on her own
In love, in loss, in failure, in growth.
A ring does not define her worth.

# The Monarch

Vibrancy of newly donned wings.
Radiance emerged from a mundane thing.
And, yet, we've missed it–
The magnificence of metamorphosis
If her details go unnoticed,
If extrinsic beauty is our sole focus.

Forgotten grandeur in her caterpillar.
In her working,
In her storing up.
Preparation for change to come–
A calculated risk,
The shedding of the old.
Exposed now.
She's vulnerable.
A goodbye to what she's known.
A decision, still, she makes
To risk it all,
To grow.

Then in the stillness of new morning,

Her sunny stripes erase.

Where once she grazed before,

Her chrysalis now hangs.

Below her surface,

Transformation.

Change is taking place.


Emerging soon,

Butterfly.


More beauty in her details

Than striations in her wings.

Artistry in her complexity,

Not in the fluttering of her wings.

How tragic to reduce something so exquisite.

Magnificent, though, minimized–

The Monarch,

And women.

# Life Beyond Nine to Five

What's the point of living if only for the weekend?

A new opportunity with each rising sun,

Choices as infinite as the stars that fill the evening sky.

May we choose to live–

Fully and freely,

On Tuesday nights,

All the same,

As Sunday mornings.

# Serotonin

It's in the mist of the waterfall at the end of a hike, and
In the way your heart feels after girl's night.

It's in the sunlight dancing on shoulders on the first day of spring, and
In watching seeds grow to vegetables, ready for harvesting.

It's in the peaceful buzz around a full table on Sunday, and
In the pitter-patter of paws following closely behind you on Monday.

It's in the gentle breeze passing through a moonlit dinner, and
In that bedtime pill that makes you feel better.

# Sisters

A lesson, still, I'm learning:
There's purpose in all things–
Maybe all the faces I see each day
Can teach me something new.

From the woman with the unshaved legs,
I learned philosophy.
She mentioned rising Gemini,
Taught about astrology.
A friendly face, though different than mine,
She chose, with me, to share good vibes.

From the religious girl dressed in a skirt,
I learned we all just need a friend.
Uncommon, but we found shared ground
In tending to gardens.
She's made for more than what she knows.
Childlike whimsy and pure-of-heart,
There's goodness in her bones.

From the bold, young girl viewed as a problem,
I learned about compassion.
That perhaps her wild and reckless ways
Are her own form of distraction.
We don't know what her life's been like,
The burdens that she carries,
But I do know that a girl her age needs more than sideways glances.

Their stories I carry one day to the next.
Though we're seemingly so different,
Something we all share:
The desire for acceptance, for community, and connection.

Maybe this journey I'm on isn't meant to find love,
But to create it wherever I go–
A purpose, I've found, is doing my part
So my sisters don't travel alone.

# Raspberry Garden

I feel closest to God
In creation,
Not a Sunday pew.

A journey since childhood,
Faith in the unseen.

I worry I've simplified Him to
Too simple things, like
The butterfly that follows each place that I go
And the color that forms as raspberries grow
In the garden I planted my first year in this home.

So much more than the things I can see, but
I know He is good
By the songs the birds sing.

# Change

Bright light plant
Stagnant
Wilting in the corner
Until
Moved to the window
Greeted by
Morning sunlight
Culture shock
At first
Uncomfortable
Until
New life
Springs forth
From
Dying limbs.

# Perspective's Lens

At thirteen years of age,
I became acutely aware of the
Surprising nature of death:
Of its finality and its sneaking up
On a person, on a family.
A life snatched away,
Leaving a funeral home full
Of the brokenhearted.

And with this new knowledge
Of just how quickly
Death can slither in and strike,
Uneasiness built a foundation firm within my mind–

Like every interaction may be my last.
Like at any moment those I love could pass.

How desperately I've tried
To memorize it all–
The sounds and smells and faces,
Pictures countless fill my phone.

It's worth it, I've learned,
To show up for your people–
Freely giving of your time,
Freely giving of yourself.

No phones at the table,
Look around, this won't last.
One day you'll blink and fifteen years have passed–
Brown hair turned to grey,
But each day we looked the same.
A slow fade with passing time.
How glad to know together was prioritized.

A sad reality that there's an end,
But how beautiful to really live,
Viewing it all through perspective's lens.

# Wildflower

She's sun-warmed and pure,

Steadfast,

Resilient,

No matter how reckless

The conditions around her.

Her beauty–

Unique.

Undervalued by those that can't see

She's more than a weed;

She's a life-giver to all those around her.

Her blooms prosper among thorns,

Vast summer fields, all the same.

Seeds tossed by the wind, but

She knows,

Wherever they land,

There is room for her

To grow.

# Faith

Sometimes I don't know where I stand with God,
The former Baptist in me is ashamed to admit.

Paradoxical, I've thought
To be given the name Faith,
Something that has never come easily.

But one thing I've decided to believe:
This name, it's for me and
It is not by accident.

Clinging to this, I'll choose to believe
That this God, He is good, and
He's not holding out on me.

# Fear

You told me not to share my words,
To blend in and think twice
Before choosing boldness.

> There are bridges you've burned,
> Foes from back then.
> They know the old you's that existed–
> Boisterous, though broken,
> At times, too outspoken.
> These demons, they'll haunt you
> If you get too far past
> These old you's that existed in years past.

Despite its best effort,
Your voice is drowned out
By the echoes of truth ringing out:

> Fear has no place
> In my rebuilt house.
> No evidence remains
> Of what existed in years past.

# Terracotta Pots

Terracotta pots line my windowsills,
Fragile plant babes fill each one.
And when they outgrow their clay homes,
I celebrate, knowing their once-shallow roots are now strong.

These growing sprouts, my teachers,
A lesson in their leaves:
To celebrate just as fully
When I outgrow the terracotta pots
No longer meant for me.

# Mishima

There's a misconception I've carried,
Equating my journey in life
To my journey in travels.
As if my growing–
Mentally and physically,
Emotionally and spiritually,
Will one day land me
On top of Mount Fuji.
The best stories,
I've since realized,
Are birthed from the unexpected.
A bus route to nowhere,
Lost in a strange town.
Adapting, not arriving.
The growing never stops.
And no amount of destination travel
Equates to heart work.

# Alive

Standing in line to pay respects,
Pictures pass by–
A life well lived, displayed on screen.
I watched while reminiscing with
A friend I haven't lately seen.
She asks about what's new and
I extend the same to her.
Of all the things to ask,
I found it funny that she chose:
*"Why do you like hiking?"*
The line inched forward,
The pictures scrolled by,
And all I knew to say was that
It makes me feel alive.

# Color Theory

Value neither gained, nor lost
With exhibit passersby.
Critiquing, admiring,
But each one, noticing.

Some prefer abstract works of art;
Some are moved by avant-garde.

My gallery is full, but
Cohesion is not within my frames.
Warm Sedona sunsets and
South Carolina autumns
Hang right next to
Melancholy murals of years gone by,
Streaks of abuse cover the canvas beside.

Impressionist.
Expressionist.
A whirlwind of brushstrokes:
Each one telling the long story of
How it all came to be.
So, in the event
You don't like the color theory
Of me,
Please be courteous and
Keep the line moving
In this gallery.

# Unbecoming

I think my twenties have been for reinvention,
Of becoming and unbecoming,
Of challenging the things always believed,
Of searching inwardly for the truest form of me.
It's more complicated than the stereotypes,
Reckless abandon at eighteen years old,
A forgotten upbringing,
Running free.
It's introspection.
Self-discovery.
Learning my own boundaries.
It's growing comfortable in my own skin,
In my own voice,
Unapologetically unbecoming
Everything that is no longer me.

# Contradictions

She is a homebody built for exploration,

Driven by the sunshine and thunderstorms in June.

She brakes for birds, just in case, but has been known to flip one too.

Quick wit from her Daddy; strong will from her Mama.

Raised in the church house, but

Fits in better in the pub down the road.

She is equal parts tender and lionhearted,

Previously at war with her own complexities.

She has now reconciled within herself that she's content to be

A compilation of contradictions.

# Refuge

The safest people, I'm convinced,
Have known the deepest hurt.
Eyes shaped by sadness,
A heart molded with compassion.
Safe to sink in,
Exactly as you are.
No need for tidying up the ugly parts of your heart.
Warm, like a wood stove crackling.
Ears tuned in, ready to hear the cries of another–
Perhaps, a voice reminiscent of themselves back when
Hurt first found its way to them.
For all the trouble we've seen,
The ones that learn to lighten the load,
Burden carrying for another–
These are the people most healed, most alive, most free.
Like cozying up in your favorite spot on the couch,
Blanket tucked around wool-socked feet,
The sound of rain tip tapping on windows.
It's safe here.
It's home.

# Wanderer

Wild wandering
Off the beaten path.
Root grasping,
Mud sliding beneath feet
On a faintly marked trail.

Most at home in the forest,
Water rushing in the distance.
More rewarding than journeys on
Paved roads in town,
Steps guided by streetlights.
Life,
Much the same,
Sometimes lost along the way.

A quick pause–
> Remember from where you came.
> Fresh perspective on where you're going,
> Chasing something bigger than ourselves.
> One lifetime is all we get.
> More is waiting
> Beyond the picket fence lined driveway
> We are told to seek out.

# Empathy

Selfish, it seems,
To feel so heavily,
Knowing the suffering
Endured by others.

Prisoners of war.
Parents burying children.
Cancer's indiscrimination.

And here I sit.
The audacity of sadness
To creep into a life like mine.
My feelings valid,
Though my loss not as great.
Still guilty, I feel,
*To feel.*

I'll sit with my sadness,
And allow her to speak.
Then she'll be redirected,
Choosing thankfulness
In all things,
Believing there is a purpose in pain,
Even if just to learn
Empathy.

# Diet

Much emphasis we place on food we consume.
And, sure, physical health is important,
But how counterintuitive to sit at a table filled
With salad and water and stress boiling over.
Negative thoughts coursing through,
As we sit and watch the news, and
Scroll a timeline of tragedy.
Whole foods have their place,
But antioxidants can't erase
All the negativity we regularly intake.
Healthy bodies have healthy minds, healthy souls, in a balance.
Mental health is so much more than iced coffee and lit candles.
Eat your salad, drink your water, but please take time to
Sit and ponder–
What else am I feeding my soul?
Is this diet of mine helping me grow?

# My Therapist Was Right

A man I met years ago
Asked today about
A ring I used to wear
On my now empty fourth finger.
An affair, the answer I gave
Along with awkward laughter,
But no sting felt in the stomach
Once pitted with anxiety,
Gripped by pain.
I'm proud in knowing
Even while I'm still growing
What once was so heavy,
No longer a burden I carry.
My past I honor.
My healing I claim.
The work I did was not in vain.
Thank God,
It really does get better.

# *Tranquility*

In the smell of fresh scones and hot coffee on Saturday morning,
In resting in the stillness, only hearing the birds chirping,
In dinner on the floor because we've run out of chairs,
In knowing what's for me won't pass me by,
In deciding to romanticize the little things in life,
I've found tranquility.

# Cupcakes

It's 5:35 on a Monday night

I'm baking cupcakes doused in sprinkles

It's not a holiday

Or my birthday

But it's a good day

Because the sun found her smile again today and so did I

And that's reason enough to celebrate tonight.

# *Ambiguity*

A New Year's tradition,
Claiming words as my own.
Little mantras, a declaration
For the days to come.

Randomly generated,
Screenshot and they're yours:
Abundant and Lasting
Became my new words.

Initially perceived to be companion confirmation:
Lasting with another, together in abundance.
Resurrected months later from memory tucked away,
Forgotten until their time to be claimed.
Abundantly clear, now,
These words were for me,
Not with another, but
Independently.

No matter what happened in all the days prior
May the day present and days to come be
Abundant–

    In knowing you're more than enough and
Lasting–

    Endurance for navigating your course,
    Even when the path seems daunting,
    Even when the road gets rough.

May this life be more than mundane repetition,
But for you to find your purpose within it.
More than falling in love and rising from crashes,
There's growth that accompanies the discovery of passions.

Abundant and Lasting,
Once given to me,
Now, I believe,
Are your words to claim.

# Words Like Water

Words strung together,
Poured out by others,
Like ice cold water on an August day,
Time and time again
Helped me carry on
Just a little farther
Through the blistering heat.

So if, by chance,
These words of mine
Can replenish another,
Helping them to carry on
Just a little farther,
How unfair to keep
All the water to myself,
A reservoir of hope hidden away.

# ABOUT THE AUTHOR

Kirsten Morgan is a writer, using poetry to explore love and loss, faith and mental health, and hope in everyday moments. She uses words to celebrate the heights of happiness, while also honoring the moments of darkness that shape us and our stories. She believes that a string of words can hold great power and hopes that her words can be a source of refuge and healing for her readers, just as the words of others have been for her. In addition to writing, she is employed full-time in physical therapy where she works with her patients to reduce their pain, improve their quality of life, and achieve their goals every day. In her free time, Kirsten can be found gathering around dinner tables with her family, enjoying the outdoors with her friends, and curled up on the couch at the end of the day with her cat, Emme.

Printed in Great Britain
by Amazon